Unicorn German Series ✤ Heinz Piontek

UNICORN GERMAN SERIES

HORST BIENEK
Translated by Ruth & Matthew Mead

ELISABETH BORCHERS
Translated by Ruth & Matthew Mead

GÜNTER EICH
Translated by Teo Savory

HEINZ PIONTEK
Translated by Richard Exner

Lyrik POETRY

Die Furt, 1952
Die Rauchfahne, 1953
Wassermarken, 1957
Mit einer Kranichfeder, 1962
Klartext, 1966
Tot oder, lebendig, 1971
Gesammelte Gedichte, 1975

Prosa PROSE

Vor Augen, 1955
Kastanien aus dem Feuer, 1963
Windrichtungen, 1963
Die mittleren Jahre, 1967
Aussenaufnahmen, 1968
Liebeserklärungen in Prosa, 1969
Die Erzählungen, 1971
Helle Tage anderswo, 1973

Essay ESSAYS

Buchstab — Zauberstab, 1959
Männer die Gedichte machen, 1970

Übersetzungen TRANSLATIONS

John Keats: Gedichte, 1960

Anthologien ANTHOLOGIES

Neue deutsche Erzählgedichte, 1964
Augenblicke unterwegs:
    Deutsche Reiseprosa unserer Zeit, 1968
Deutsche Gedichte seit 1960, 1972

UNICORN GERMAN SERIES

HEINZ PIONTEK

Alive or Dead

Translated by Richard Exner

Greensboro: Unicorn Press: 1975

The translator gratefully acknowledges the assistance in his
work of Wm. Scott McLean.

Some of these translations were originally published in
Dimension.

Tot oder lebendig, here issued under the title of *Alive or Dead,*
was originally published, in its entirety, in Germany in 1971
and was awarded the Eichendorff Prize of that year. The
English translation and its publication have been, in part,
sponsored by The Bavarian Academy of Fine Arts (Munich)
and the Government of the Federal Republic of Germany; it is
issued by Unicorn Press for the occasion of the fiftieth birth-
day of its author, Heinz Piontek, as Volume IV in the Unicorn
German Series.

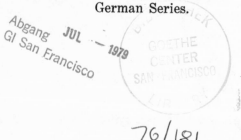

Horseman, pass by!
W. B. Yeats

CONTENTS

Introduction by Richard Exner

Biographical Notes

Heinz Piontek

Piontek's bibliography speaks for itself. If one adds the collections which he assembled and introduced one can summarize: a writer of great distinction, primarily a poet, an inspired artificer whose command of language, metaphor and symbol is astonishing; an author whose every new book opens new linguistic and mental territory, a free-lance artist who has created an audience for himself, a fashioner rather than a follower of tastes. Puzzled critics have called him a "modern classic"; for the time being, he is himself and believes that man's estate must constantly be delineated, defended, summarized and praised, lest it be brutalized or wasted. The writer, also, as magician: while the spell lasts, we exist in decency and responsibility; afterwards, a metaphor, a sentence, a landscape may remind us that if we do not write our own code of human conduct, no one else will.

Twelve years ago, Piontek wrote: "I am sometimes called a loner. This is correct inasmuch as I have not joined any 'school'. But this fact should be used neither to judge nor to recommend me. To be by myself is a matter of personal make-up, of predilection, of temperament. I feel a sense of community, through admiration and consent, with many dead and some living poets."

The collection ALIVE OR DEAD, from which the contents of this book have been chosen, is Piontek's sixth volume of poetry. His earlier poetry seems to lie far behind despite similarity in theme and attitude. He X-rays his era, its slogans and ideologies; he states some unpleasant truths. He is eloquent but not wordy. He has become a master at cutting his own poems to the bone. His vocabulary of essentials and essences is distilled from a vast repository of poetic language, informed by tradition. Pathos is rare; during the last years there is increasing evidence of a benign scepticism, of measured irony. Yet, when a remembered landscape, for example, pushes his visions into the truth, he does not need a long hymnic line to express praise.

Heinz Piontek is, as this volume of originals and translations shows, an extraordinarily conscious poet, awake and conscientious; to him, his accomplished craft is neither routine nor sullen.

Richard Exner

Im Wasser

Unter Badenden
bin ich als Schiffbrüchiger
nicht kenntlich.

Wo bleibt meine Zukunft?
Über mir, unter mir
nichts.

Mit letzter Kraft forme ich Worte.
Von meinem Mund
ist nichts abzulesen.

Ein halbtoter Fisch,
der zu schreien versucht,
das sieht lustig aus.

Submerged

Among bathers
I am not noticed
as shipwrecked.

What about my future?
Above me, below me
there is nothing.

With ultimate effort I mouth words.
My lips reveal
nothing.

A half-dead fish
attempting a scream;
that is hilarious.

Ankommen

Windgeplagt,
mit Schneehöhlen im Gesicht.

Aussentemperatur
ein Minus-Wort.

Endlich das Blut klopfen hören,
aufstampfen,

wenn Schloss und Angel
die Sicht freigeben:

auf breitgetretene Asche
toter Öfen,
das Gespenst des Feuers.

Arrived

Windtormented,
snowcaves in the face.

Outside temperature
a minus word.

Finally to hear the blood pound,
to stomp,

when lock and hinge
bare the sight:

flattened ashes
of dead furnaces,
the spectre of fire.

Totenlitanei für von der Vring

Hinter den Wasserfarben verregneter Gärten
hinter Kavaliershäusern Schuluhren Kanälen
hinter dem Heu und Stroh von Blumen
hinter Sommer und Herbst

hinter dem Wort Flandern
hinter den Lippen einer Schwäbin
hinter blauem Nebel wie der Sage von weissen
treibenden Haaren und dem ans Ufer gezogenen
Körper

hinter Starrsinn Wahn Liebe
hinter dem voll bezahlten Preis
hinter einem Wall an der Weser

werden dich auferwecken
die silberkehligen Hörner deiner Gedichte

Litany for the Dead Poet von der Vring

Behind the watercolors of raindrenched gardens
behind patrician houses schoolclocks canals
behind the hay and straw of flowers
behind summer and autumn

behind the word Flanders
behind the lips of a Swabian woman
behind the blue mist as behind the legend
of white floating hair and the body pulled ashore

behind obstinacy illusion love
behind the fully paid price
behind a dike at the river Weser

they will awaken you
the silverthroated cornets of your poems

Nachtwind

Hinter uns das Land,
das wir mit Wörtern furchten.

Ihr und ich.

Geblieben ist die Stoppel.
Schwalbenkot. Im Dunkel die Gänge
mit gesenkter Fackel.

Nachtwind, Nachtwind:
Wie hohl klingen die Tennen!

Wer wird mit mir aufstehn
störrisch wie ein Maultier, den Kopf senken,
weitermachen?

Ich rufe vor herabgelassenen Jalousien,
Türen ohne Schilder.
Schaue auf gestrichene Segel.
Ich erschrecke.

Ja, meine aufgescheuchten Schritte, diese Stimme
eines hartnäckigen Sperlings,
nicht bereit, sich zu trennen von dem,
was sie weiss,
und das getrocknete Salz im Gesicht:

Nightwind

Behind us the earth
we furrowed with words.

You and I.

What's left is the stubble.
Swallow's dung. The passages in darkness
with a lowered torch.

Nightwind, nightwind:
the threshing floors resound so hollow!

Who will rise with me
stubborn as a mule, lower his head
and keep going?

I cry before lowered shutters,
before doors without nameplates.
I look upon struck sails.
I am frightened.

Yes, my startled steps, this voice
of a persistent sparrow,
unwilling to tear itself
from what it knows,
the dried streaks of salt in my face:

Sollte, wer übrigbleibt,
sich nicht lieber verstecken?

Nachtwind, Nachtwind,
Kurier:

Steht es fest,
dass ich der Letzte bin?

Da sind sie, unwiderruflich,
eure falben Lider,
die sich nicht von selbst geschlossen haben.
Eure begrabenen Hoffnungen, Schlussstriche,
letzten zornigen Atemzüge.

Nein, die Rede von euch soll nicht aufhören,
nur weil man satt geworden ist
von eurem Getreide.

Helft mir,
holt ihre Flinten aus dem Herbst,
ihre Heimat aus dem Rauch,
was sie versprachen, verfehlten,
von unseren Grenzen

und legt alles zu den Jahren,
zu denen man stehen muss—

should he, who is finally left,
not rather take cover?

Nightwind, nightwind,
messenger:

is it certain
that I am the last one?

There they are, irrevocable,
your fallow lids
which have not closed by themselves.
Your buried hopes, final accounts,
your last angry breaths.

No, they shall go on talking about you
even though they have had more than enough
of the grain you threshed.

Help me,
get their guns from the autumn,
their home from the smoke,
their promises and failures
from our borders

and add all this to the years
to which we must be true—

wie der Löwenzahn zum Grummet,
das Steingut zum Feuer,
tot oder lebendig.

Aber was weiter?

Äussert die stehengelassene Kiefer,
was sie zu tun gedenkt
bis zur nächsten Rodung?

Oben im Dunkel,
wo sich die Krone verliert,
im unbeherrschten Geräusch über der Erde

nimmt sie alle Nadeln zusammen,
damit es nicht abreisst,
das trockne halblaute Klirren.

Nachtwind, Nachtwind:

Dass wir nichts Besseres versuchen können
als treusein -

was auch immer das heisst.

as the weed is true to the hay,
the crockery to the fire,
dead or alive.

But what next?

Does the spared pine say
what it intends to do
before the next felling?

Above in the dark
where the crown disappears,
in the uncontrolled noise over the earth,

it holds on to all its needles
so that the dry subdued clanging
will not cease.

Nightwind, nightwind:

all we can do is attempt
to be faithful—

whatever that means.

Merkwürdig

Stehen. Gehen.

Noch am Abend
mit der Zuversicht
vom Morgen

auf des Messers Spitze.

Und die platonische
Liebe, die Wolken.

Freudenfeuer,

wo durch die Gebüsche
der Nacht Wer-da hallt.

Worth Noting

Standing. Walking.

In the evening
still the confidence
of the morning

on the razor's edge.

And platonic
love, the clouds.

Bonfires,

where through the thicket
resounds the night's "Who goes there."

Unter den Alpen

1

Schlechtwetter wie Heusträhnen,
von den Bäumen hängend.

Und die Parolen: Dass Ja nicht Ja heisst,
mir ein Strick gedreht wird -

Doch wirklicher: Was ich versäumte,
in den Rauchfang schrieb -

Vergeblichkeit:
unsre Garrotte -

Nichts mehr hör ich
übers Gebirge.

Below the Alps

1

Bad weather hanging like hay
from the trees.

And the passwords: that yes is not yes,
that I'm readied for the noose—

More precisely: what I neglected,
what went up in smoke—

Futility:
our garrotte—

No more messages
from across the mountains.

2

Ein Apfel, grünschalig.
Tiroler Wein dazu.

Es hört auf zu regnen.
Gestern war ich verzweifelt.

Und schon klärt sich die Luft.
Mein Mut wächst.

Im voraus
zerstöre ich Wörter,

mit denen ich segeln könnte
übers Gebirge.

2

An apple, with a green peel.
And a glass of Tyrolean wine.

It stops raining.
Yesterday I was desperate.

Now the air is beginning to clear.
My courage grows.

And in advance
I destroy words,

with which I could sail
across the mountains.

Schreiben

Gedachte Linien:
Flugschneisen.

Wörter als Leitton
in der Ohrmuschel.

Möglichkeiten,
die Häfen zu erreichen.

Man setzt sein Leben
aufs Spiel.

Writing

Imagined lines:
airways.

Words as the radio-beam
in the auricle.

Chances
to reach port.

You stake
your life.

Nach Jahren

Die Masse Wasser
bei Ulm:

Wiedersehen mit etwas
schwer Durchschaubarem,

was schon immer sich wälzte
wer weiss wohin,

am Ende
nicht zu beirren -

und ich: dieselben
Fragen vor mir herschiebend,

mit menschlicher Ausdauer,
das ist klar,

noch immer unruhig und
etwas zu hastig -

auch das Bett,
das an meins erinnert:

gewisse Orte,
wo unsere Auflösung beginnt.

Years Later

Masses of water
near Ulm:

Reunion with something
barely transparent,

always flowing
who knows where,

ultimately
imperturbable—

and I: turning over
the same questions,

with human endurance,
that's clear,

still restive and
a little too hurried—

and the riverbed,
not unlike mine:

certain places,
where our disintegration sets in.

31

Zu alten Gedichten

Der Ausdruck der Äste
bei zwölf Grad Kälte -
wer schrieb davon?

Berief sich auf den
unbestechlichen Schnee?

Wer suchte was klarzumachen
an einer Schwanzfeder,
die durchs Weisse stob?

Ich verziehe die Lippen
über mich.

Deutlicher als im Sommer
sehe ich nur
den Russ fallen.

Doch diese Versuche,
festzuhalten,
was niemand gesehen hat.

Die strahlende Gestalt
des Eises.

Concerning Old Poems

The expression of treelimbs
in ten degree weather—
who has written about it?

Cited the testimony
of the incorruptible snow?

Who has tried to explain something
with the help of a tailfeather
that rushed through whiteness?

My lips are distorted with contempt
for myself.

More distinctly than during the summer
I see only
the soot fall.

Yet these attempts
to record
what no one has seen.

The brilliant appearance
of ice.

Vor dem Gewitter am 21. August 1968

Schwalben leuchten auf
in grosser Höhe.

Kurze Schläge. Segeln
vor einer dunklen Wand.

Unerbittlich wird das Wort
Atmosphäre
zum Zentnergewicht.

Aber die Federleichten
halten den Kurs.

Ich sehe, wie sie
die geladene Luft durchstossen.
Glühend.

Before the Thunderstorm on August 21, 1968

Swallows are luminous
at great height.

Short wingbeats. Sailing
against a background of black.

Relentlessly the word
atmosphere
becomes a hundredweight.

But these featherlight creatures
hold their course.

I see them
pierce the charged air.
Blazing.

Utopische Gedichte

1

Bürger Krieg, am Ende
wirst du der letzte
Bürger sein.

2

Strassenschlachten zwischen den Farben,
den Geburtstagen, den Geschlechtsteilen,
den Seiten ein und desselben Buches.
Kein Pardon.

3

Städte, ihr werdet wieder
durchschaubar werden.
Der Traum vom Einfachen geht
durchs Feuer.

4

In verbarrikadierten Häusern
nimmt das Geld noch einmal
die Gestalt der Renaissance an.

5

Strick und Grube
für bevorzugte Fälle.
Uns wird man liegenlassen
auf dem Pflaster.

Utopian Poems

1

Citizen war, in the end
you will be
the last citizen.

2

Streetfights between the races,
the birthdays, the genitals,
the pages of one and the same book.
No pàrdon given.

3

Cities, you will again
become transparent.
The dream of simple things
is tested by fire.

4

In barricaded homes
once again money will
take on the form of the Renaissance.

5

Noose and pit
for the happy few.
We will be left
lying on the pavement.

6

Ja der Frieden,
nur mit Gewalt zu erfahren.

7

Schönes Leben
der Banditen,
die den Bartspitzen ihres Hauptmanns
die Rätsel überlassen,
mit Bräuten auf den Dächern kampieren.

8

Dann wissen wieder
die Unbelesenen mehr.

9

Auf dem Lande
wird man zittern.

10

Defätist!

6

Oh and peace,
only to be known by force.

7

The marvelous life
of bandits,
who leave their problems
in the beard of their captain
and camp with their brides on roofs.

8

Then the unlettered
will be learnèd again.

9

They will tremble
in the country.

10

Defeatist!

Bäume

für Alfred Focke

Ihr ja ihr.

Ruhig auf der dunklen
Erde fussend.

Doch verwundbar
wie wir,

die wir uns vorwärts-
kämpfen müssen.

Nützlich oder
einfach schön

und immer etwas
Neues bedeutend.

So wachsen:

In die Höhe,
in die Tiefe

und mit
ausgebreiteten Armen.

Trees

for Alfred Focke

Yes you.

Silently rooted in
the dark earth.

Yet as vulnerable
as we

who must fight on.

Useful or
simply beautiful

and always signifying
something new.

To grow like this:

into the heights,
into the depths

and with
arms spread wide.

Singen

Erfahrungen mit dem Himmelskörper,
zurückgeführt
auf einen einfachen Schmerz.

Etwas wird laut,
das uns entspricht.

Wenige klare Töne.

So transponierte jemand in einer Wiener Gasse
den Juniregen.

Unsere Befreiung liegt
in der Luft.

Vor hellen aber gezeichneten Augen
erscheint ein Umriss.

Die Unerbittlichkeit
gibt es nicht.

Song

Experiences with the celestial body,
reduced to
a simple pain.

Suddenly a sound
that touches us.

A few clear notes.

In this way someone transposed the June rain
on a street in Vienna.

Our liberation lies
in the air.

An outline appears
before clear but marked eyes.

Inexorability
does not exist.

Madrigal

In unserm Winterquartier
treiben wir den Winter aus

Treiben wir den Winter aus
an Rhein und Donau
auf dem verdorbnen Feld

Beisst auch wie Schrot der Schnee
Wehr dich nur Antichrist

Wir treiben Feuer bergan

Madrigal

In our winter quarters
we expel the winter

Drive the winter out
near Rhine and Danube
on the spoilt field

And if the snow bites like shot
defend yourself, Antichrist

We drive fire up the mountain

Fliegendes Blatt

Getäuscht
Getäuscht

Du bist nicht
du

Zur Zeit
des Sternezersingens

Getäuscht

Zur Zeit
wenn die Mörder ausruhn

Getäuscht

Des Nachts
beim Schleichen zu knarrenden Schiffen

Oder

du warst nicht
du

Flying Leaflet

Deceived
Deceived

You are not
yourself

When the stars
are sung to shreds

Deceived

When the assassins
relax

Deceived

At night
silently moving toward creaking ships

Or

you were not
yourself

Einfache Sätze aus dem Jahr 68

1

Jemand lässt durchblicken, dass er
gegen die Zeit ist.

Jemand protestiert mit seinem Transparent
gegen Transparente.

Andere haben gleichschenklige
Dreiecke im Kopf.

Die Aufklärung nimmt zu.
Es wird dunkel.

Neue Bücher ergeben neue
Transparente.

Die Zukunft soll
rothaarig sein.

Über die Zukunft
sprechen wir morgen.

Simple Statements Made in '68

1

Someone intimates that he
is against the times.

Someone carries a banner
protesting banners.

Others have equilateral
triangles in their heads.

Enlightenment grows apace.
It is getting dark.

New books beget new
banners.

The future, I hear,
is a redhead.

We'll discuss the future
tomorrow.

2

Jemand weiss Bescheid.
Er ist Schüler.

Alte Leute erzählen immer nur
alte Geschichten.

Ein Seminarist und eine Wucherin
in St. Petersburg:

Klassiker, gut für
Kreuzworträtsel.

Nichts ist so lästig wie
was gut ist.

Man kann nicht immer nur
auf Fliegen Jagd machen.

Mode wird bald
die Axt unterm Mantel.

Alle sprechen vom Überfluss.

Es soll wieder
überflüssige Menschen geben.

2

Someone knows what's up.
He's a student.

Old people never tell anything
but old tales.

A seminarian and a usurer
in St. Petersburg:

The classics: splendid stuff
for crossword puzzles.

Nothing is quite so annoying
as what is good.

You cannot always
just chase flies.

To carry a hatchet under your coat
will soon come in style.

Everyone talks of affluence.

I hear there are
superfluous people again.

3

Täglich verliert jemand seine Unschuld
unter Schlagstöcken.

Täglich verstehen wir uns weniger.

Tageszeitungen kommen noch
täglich.

Der Frieden eine Komödie.

Es hat keinen Sinn mehr
auszuwandern.

Einfache Sätze werden
nicht einfacher.

3

Everyday the nightsticks rob
someone's innocence.

Every day we understand each other less.

Dailies are still delivered
every day.

Peace is a comedy.

To emigrate
no longer serves any purpose.

Simple statements don't get any
simpler.

Ich, Anton Pawlowitsch

simuliere Gesundheit,
putze meinen Zwicker,
beobachte die Unkurierbaren.

Als Einziger meiner Gilde
sah ich das Weisse im Auge von Deportierten,
notierte Schreie, Knüppelwunden,
die Wärmequelle des Mondes
auf der Eisfläche Sachalin.

Gott stärke mein Gedächtnis,
denn schreibe ich nicht schon wieder
von sich langweilenden Mädchen,
verwöhnten Gaunern, grünen und
grauen Dummköpfen

und habe die Stirn,
demnächst auch noch über
ein Feld voll Kirschbäume zu schreiben?

Diese Namenslisten, Hinweise
auf Landgüter, die ich
ans Theater sende.

I, Anton Pavlovich

simulate health,
clean my pince-nez
and observe the incurables.

The only one of my branch
I saw the white in the eyes of deported men,
noted screams and flogging wounds,
the heatsource of the moon
on the icy plains of the Sakhalin Islands.

My God, strengthen my memory:—
I'm at it again, writing
about bored girls,
pampered cheats, green
and grey idiots

and I will have the nerve one of these days
to write about
a cherry orchard!

These lists full of names, and
references to estates, which I send
to the theatre.

Die Wahrheit
darf nicht auffallen,
ich mache grosse Pausen
zwischen den Worten.

So verdiene ich schwitzend
mit durchgefallenen Stücken.

Wenn mich die Alten loben,
dann mangels Besserem,
die Jungen verhöhnen meine weissen
Handschuhe, sie wollen
Blut sehen.

Schon höre ich sie
rund um das
ausgehobene Loch:

Och, wäre er nicht so
unentschieden gewesen!

Als hätte ich nicht
von Anfang an
gegen die Lüge protestiert.

The truth must not
be conspicuous,
I put long pauses
between the words.

I sweat and I earn a living
writing rejected plays.

If the older generation praises me
it's strictly *faute de mieux*;
the young people ridicule my white
gloves, they want to see
blood.

I can hear them already,
standing around the
excavated hole:

God, if he had only
committed himself!

As if I hadn't protested
against lies
from the very beginning.

Nicht mehr gewillt

Ist es wahr,
wir verknöchern?

Dauert der Frieden
schon zu lange?

Unser mit Blutverlusten,
Salz, Nerven erkaufter,
windiger Frieden?

Ja, rechnet nur mit uns
ab, uns
Feiglingen:

geschlagen, gebrannt
wie wir sind -

und nicht mehr gewillt,
die Gewalt

noch einmal
auf unsere Schultern
zu heben.

No longer willing

Is it true
that we have become so hardened?

Has peace really
lasted too long?

Our shoddy peace,
bought with blood,
salt and nerves?

Yes, settle up with
us cowards:

beaten and burnt —

And no longer willing
to shoulder

violence
once again.

aus Neue Parolen

Der Schatten meiner Feder wirft ein bezeichnendes Licht.

Ah ihr Gedichte, die ihr die Ehre hattet, für Menschen einzuspringen. Jetzt müsst ihr Steinen aus der Seele sprechen.

Verzweifelt bitte ich um den Mut der Verzweiflung.

Glück haben: keinen Schuss Pulver wert sein.

Ich lege die Maske ab. Niemand erkennt mich.

Schwalben kann man vom Himmel herunterholen. Doch kann man sie zwingen, nur in einer Richtung zu fliegen?

Den Kampf zwischen Leiden und Tod wird das Leiden gewinnen.

Der Hang steiler, das Wegende schärfer, das Blau reiner: Schritt um Schritt.

Sprache ist Luft für mich.

Unanfechtbarkeit im Luftleeren. Die letzte Klarheit ist nichtssagend.

Das Klare ist nicht das Unmögliche, sondern das Unmögliche ist das Klare.

Das Schweigen verrät dich.

Wörter, bis zum Hals in Wörtern.

from New Passwords

The shadow of my pen throws a telling
light.

Oh yes you poems of mine that had the honor
to take a man's place. Now you must speak for
stones.

In despair I ask for the courage of despair.

To be lucky: not to be worth a bullet.

I take off my mask. No one recognizes me.

You can shoot swallows out of the sky. But can
you force them to fly in only one direction?

Suffering will be triumphant in the battle
between suffering and death.

So much steeper the incline, so much sharper
the path's end, so much purer the blue:
step by step.

Language is air for me.

Unassailability in a vacuum. The last clarity
tells us nothing.

The lucid is not the impossible; it is the
impossible which is the lucid.

Silence betrays you.

Words, up to your neck in words.

HEINZ PIONTEK is one of Germany's most distinguished contemporary writers, whose work, except for several excellent publications in *Dimension*, has until now been neglected in this country. Now Unicorn Press presents a volume of his poetry, his first in English translation, in celebration of the author's fiftieth birthday, and in conjunction with other publications, in Germany, for the same occasion. The translation, by Richard Exner, himself a fine poet as well as an eminent scholar, was made in collaboration with the author.

Heinz Piontek was born in Upper Silesia and has lived for some years in Munich, where he has been a free-lance author since 1948. He was awarded the Berlin Literature Prize in 1957 and held the Villa Massimo Fellowship in 1960. He is a member of the Bavarian Academy of Fine Arts. Six books of his poetry were published previous to the publication by Hoffmann and Campe of his *Collected Poetry* in 1975. His prose works include essays, short stories and radio plays, as well as his novel, *The Middle Years*, which was acclaimed in Germany as an important avant-garde work.

RICHARD EXNER teaches German and European Literature at the University of California, Santa Barbara. He has written extensively on the Austrian poet, Hugo von Hofmannsthal, and has published poems, prose, and translations in both German and English; one of his poems was issued by Unicorn Press at Christmas, 1972.